A VERY FINE
CAT INDEED

A Very Fine Cat Indeed

A DRAMATIC MONOLOGUE

ROBINSAIKIA

Poussin Paris

Robin Saikia was born in 1962 and educated at Winchester College. He wrote *The Venice Lido*, a literary and historical guide to Venice's beach resort. He compiled *Blue Guide Literary Companion London*, an anthology of poetry and prose excerpts written in and about London. He also wrote *The Red Book: The Membership List of The Right Club*, *Blue Guide Hay-on-Wye*, and *Blue Guide Italy Food Companion: Phrasebook & Miscellany*. He was editor of *The Horn Book: A Victorian Sex Manual*.

ISBN 978-1-905742-96-7
First Printing, 2020
Poussin Publications
Paris

CONTENTS

*In memory of Menelao, another
Very Fine Cat Indeed*

INTRODUCTION

When I first had the idea of writing a dramatic monologue about Hodge, I began by trying to found out what, if anything, had been previously been attempted in this line. Whereas Hodge has made various appearances in books and essays, to the best of my knowledge he has not figured in drama, save for one notable exception. I found, initially with dismay, that he had been included in *Human Wishes*, an unfinished play by Samuel Beckett, who by any standards is a hard act to follow. I was relieved to learn that this play is largely about Johnson's relationship with Hester Thrale and her circle, and that Hodge puts in only a fleeting appearance. I was struck in passing by Beckett's stage direction for the appearance of Hodge: *"asleep, if possible"*. This triggered recurrent nightmares about the pitfalls of putting a real cat on stage. as was Beckett's intention. I therefore resolved to play safe and write this monologue as a memorial piece, in which Johnson mourns his late friend. Thus, two boxes were resolutely ticked – no question of cats in the theatre, and a monologue resolutely in *memento mori* mode, eminently suitable for a piece about Johnson.

The monologue is a blend of real and imagined events. For example, Johnson's account of his childhood trip to London to see Queen Anne is real, and recounted in his own words. The appearance of the American, Upstead, is real too, though whether Hodge was present at the encounter is not recorded – and thus Upstead's flippant remark about the relative blackness of Francis Barber and Hodge is my own embroidery. Boswell's well-known account of Johnson and Hodge has been partially adapted. Mrs. Adams and Mrs. Knowles existed and were on the periphery of Johnson's circle, and the heated exchange about St. Paul certainly took place. The story of Hodge and Annie the beggarwoman is imaginary, though Johnson's very real tirade against withholding charity from beggars is reproduced in full. The scene at the oyster-cart in Porridge-island is also my own invention, though I link it to a real and very distressing event, when Johnson made a pilgrimage to Uttoxeter in an attempt to atone for what he saw as his monstrous disloyalty to his father. We know that Johnson visited Christopher Smart in St. Luke's Hospital for Lunatics. We also know that Jeremy Bentham saw Johnson at the Mitre Tavern at some unspecified point in the early 1780s, but we do not know for certain whether they actually had a conversation. Though the exchange is therefore imagined, the Bentham animal stories are real and are recorded in Bowring's memoir of his life. Busby and Proctor, the animal impressionists, are real too. As to overall style, Johnson enthusiasts will readily recognize the passages directly quoted from Johnson or Boswell. For the imaginary passages, I assembled a large compendium of words and phrases drawn from the breadth of Johnson's work, then redeployed them to fit the narrative. Thus, for example, the phrase "spritely mien" is borrowed from an essay in *The Rambler* about foppishness and dandyism. Here, it is reapplied in a description of Hodge. I hope that the end result is seamless, and that readers may feel able to forgive what they may perceive as the occasional inadvertent solecism.

I have included five brief Appendices: I, Percival Stockdale's poem, 'An Elegy on the Death of Dr. Johnson's Favourite Cat'; II, Susan Coolidge's poem, 'Dr. Johnson and Hodge His Cat'; III, an excerpt from Leigh Hunt's essay, 'The Cat by the Fire'; IV, Christopher Smart's 'Jeoffry' from *Jubilate Agno*; V, Jeremy Bentham's animal anecdotes. If the monologue is performed, I would like to think that some or all of these pieces might precede or surround the performance. At all events they seem to be fitting and, I hope, useful additions. Readers might also be interested in exploring the late Yvonne Skargon's excellent book, *Lily and Hodge and Dr. Johnson*, which contains quotations from the *Dictionary* interspersed with woodcuts by the author. Finally, if any readers find themselves in London, they should certainly visit Johnson's house in Gough Square, and take in Jon Bickley's excellent sculpture of Hodge, installed outside the museum. Bickley modelled the sculpture on his own cat, Thomas Henry, and made sure the installation was of a suitable height to be "huggable".

Lately, visitors have taken to leaving oyster shells by the statue as tokens of good luck, a wholly appropriate and moving ritual.

Robin Saikia

May 2020

A VERY FINE CAT INDEED

I

[*Towards midnight, November 1783. Dr Johnson's house in London. Music, The Maid of Bedlam. An arm-chair and table centre stage left, a ball of twine and a rag-doll cat on the table. A sideboard centre stage right with decanter and glasses. Hodge's basket, with blanket, downstage centre right. Enter Dr Johnson. Music fades.*]

JOHNSON [*Standing downstage centre, unaware of the audience.*]: Let this not be a dark and melancholy night in London. Let it rather be morning in the Highlands, and let me sit by the bank of a stream. Let there be trees to whisper over my head, and a clear rivulet to flow at my feet. Let the day be calm, the air soft, and all be solitude. Before me, and on either side, let there be high hills to protect me, and defend my eyes from the contemplation of dreadful horizons. Grant me this, and I will spend the hour well, in mourning of my poor cat Hodge. [*Picks up basket.*] This was his crib, his basket, his bed. Now he is gone. [*Replaces basket, sits in armchair, closes eyes, clasps hands as if in prayer.*]

I give thanks for my Hodge. He was black as night, soft as sable, with eyes of emerald. He would frolic before me, in dances and serenades, at tournaments and adventures. [*unclasps hands, turns attention to props*] This was his ball of twine to pat and chase. And this a doll he kept, but liked not much. When I teased him, his capers mimicked the softness of foppery, the swell of insolence, the liveliness of levity, the solemnity of grandeur. By turns he practised the sprightly trip, the stately stalk, the formal strut, the lofty mien. When done, he slept, reposing on my breast. His rumbles of content, and warm black fur, thawed the frost of my soul, and dispelled the torpor of despondency. I loved him. He was a fine cat. A very fine cat indeed. [*Johnson now engages the audience, rising from the chair and walking to the sideboard where he pours a glass of wine. Stands, near table.*]

Forgive me, friends. I live now in a melancholy way, as you may observe. My servant, Francis Barber, tends me well, but Hodge is gone. My old friend Mr. Levet is dead, who lived with me in the house, and was useful and companionable. Mrs. Desmoulins is gone away. And Mrs. Williams is so much decayed, that she can add little to another's gratifications. Dear Boswell, with some of his troublesome kindness, has reminded me that next week falls my birthday. The return of my birthday, if I ever remember it, fills me with thoughts which are the general care of humanity to escape. Yet, let us be of cheer, for night should be the kingdom of ease and gaiety. For Hodge's sake, we must find means by which cheerfulness may here be promoted, and friendship established. So I will begin by telling you how I came to love cats.

When I was a little boy and sick with scrofula, I was taken to London, to be touched for the evil by Queen Anne. I always retained some memory of this journey, though I was then but a little more than two years old. In London we stayed at Nicholson's famous bookshop. I remember a little dark room behind the kitchen, with a hole in the floor, into which I once slipped my leg. I seem to remember, that I played with a string and a bell, which my cousin Isaac Johnson gave me. There was an orange cat with a white collar, and a dog, called Chops, that leaped over a stick. Chops sprang about, and frightened me, though he meant no ill. Yet the orange cat was soft and let me touch him. I resolved I would one day keep a cat. In my infant mind, I fancied that Queen Anne might find me one, but she did not. [*Stands, walks downstage centre left.*]

After much dolour and vicissitude, with which I shall not task you, I came to manhood and kept cats. The cats I kept I liked, but they were changeable. Ruff was handsome, but of loose manners and turbulent disposition. Abby was affectionate, though in truth it seemed but a stratagem for her betterment. I kept two cats in Lichfield, that Davey Garrick knew and loved, Sam and Tibs. But they waged wars, each incessantly in schemes to intercept the happiness of the other. And yet, we live in hope. The natural flights of the human mind are not from pleasure to pleasure, but from hope to hope. And so I went from cat to cat, they lived and died, and how I came by Hodge I should relate. [*Returns to armchair.*]

II

There are, in this world, pious women of gentle breeding, somewhat past the prime of life, but irradiated with determined zeal. They may still be found in the precincts of cathedrals and churches, eager to assist and advise the clergy. You may know such women. I knew two such nearby, Mrs. Knowles and Mrs. Adams, whose daily projection was to perform small acts of kindness for the wretched.

In Fleet Street, there always sat an old beggar-woman, Annie, to whom one evening I gave half-pence, in sight of Mrs. Knowles and Mrs. Adams.

"Why sir," said Mrs. Knowles, "she'll only lay it out in gin or tobacco."

"She will!" said Mrs. Adams.

"Dear Ladies," I returned, "Why should she be denied such sweeteners of her existence? it is surely very savage to refuse her every possible avenue to pleasure, reckoned too coarse for our own acceptance. Life is a pill which none of us can bear to swallow without gilding; yet for the poor we delight in stripping it still barer, and are not ashamed to shew even visible displeasure, if ever the bitter taste is taken from their mouths." This silenced them. And through discreet enquiry and diligent observation, I found this Annie to be no slave to Dionysus. Her red and yellow dress was ragged, but clean and neat, as were her black shawl and bonnet. By night she sheltered in the attic of a baker in Angel-street. She had a little black cat, called Hephzibah, that she kept in a hessian bag and brought out with her to Fleet Street. She perpetually sang to this cat. She often sang a ballad, The Maid of Bedlam, which brought her many halfpence. I still recall it now, and how the cat was so attentive. [*Johnson sings, not very tunefully.*]

> Abroad as I was walking
> One morning in the Spring,
> I heard a maid in Bedlam
> So sweetly she did sing;
> Her chains she rattled in her hands,
> And always so sang she:
> I love my love
> Because I know he first loved me.

III

One day as I was walking, one morning in the Spring, I was accosted by Mrs. Knowles and Mrs. Adams who brought me to Annie's corner, saying nothing more than that my assistance was most promptly required. When we arrived, the black shawl was spread out on the flags, and on it Hephzibah lay. She was nursing three kitlings, one full black, and two black with pies of white upon them.

"Dr Johnson," cried Annie, "Mrs. Knowles and Mrs. Adams says you will help these poor kitlings."

Just as every moment of my life I am prepared to meet my Maker, so also every moment I have means to act upon a pressing cause.

"Madam," said I, "I will take the black kitling when his mother has reared him to sufficient growth. When I do, I will send his brothers with Francis to a good woman in Hertfordshire, where they are sure to be kindly used."

And in time I brought Hodge, the full black kitling, to my house, in the company of Mrs. Knowles and Mrs. Adams. Lodge and Podge were carried into the country by Francis, where they sate happily in a great barn.

You may know that my servant, Francis Barber, is a negro. One day, soon after the installation of Hodge, Boswell brought here a Mr. Upstead, lately from our American colonies. Francis was sporting with Hodge upon the hearth.

"Why, Dr Johnson," said Upstead, "I know not which be the blacker, thy servant or thy cat!", this in full hearing of poor Francis, and Hodge.

"That, sir," said I, "is a question that I fear you may soon be at full Liberty to determine yourself, without the benefit of direction either from me or from our Sovereign Majesty King George."

It is worth remarking, that we hear the loudest yelps for liberty among the drivers of negroes. Of black men, the numbers are too great who are now repining under cruelty. Boswell poured wine for us. I took up Hodge under my arm and proposed a toast: "Here's to the next insurrection of the negroes in the West Indies." That silenced Upstead.

IV

Despite his collision with Upstead, little Hodge grew well. I have often remarked to Boswell, that much may be made of a Scotchman, if he be caught young. The same is true of a cat. You have, as it were, the tabula rasa. There are, as I learned after much error, but two precepts for the education of a young cat. You should neither glut him with delicacies nor grant him the softness of perpetual affability. This regimen in place, permit him toys, to stretch his mind and body, and gladden his waking hours. Here is a ball of twine that he much loved. Here is a rag-doll cat that he loved not, though it was fashioned by his patrons, Mrs. Knowles and Mrs. Adams. As to this rag-doll cat, he would but look on it a while in careless insolence, then turn his rear upon it.

One morning Mrs. Knowles said, "Sir, I trust the rag-doll cat goes well with Hodge? How he must caper with it!"

"Ay, madam," said I. "He likes it well enough." I did not wish to disappoint, for I saw in her good Christian eyes the full gallery of hope and faith, and love. But ah, the ball of twine. When but a weak, black tuft of fur upon this table, he urged it laboriously hither and thither, an infant Sisyphus. Later it was a planet for him, and he a capricious Jove to spin it through his universe. When he was grown, and turned a hunter, it was for him a rat on which to pounce, a mouse to run to ground. When old he kept it by him still, and was jealous of it.

His antipathy to the rag-doll cat always brought to mind a man who said to me, "What think you, sir? Ihave got for my baby the tale of Goody Two Shoes by Mr. Newberry. It sells with great velocity and in numerous editions."

"Depend on it, Sir," said I, "Babies do not want to hear about babies; they like to be told of giants and castles, and of somewhat which can stretch and stimulate their little minds. As to the velocity of sales, remember always that the parents buy the books, and that the children never read them." That silenced him.

V

One day, as we watched Hodge caper, Boswell re-marked that the poet Kit Smart had called his cat, one Jeoffrey, a servant of the living God. "Ay sir," said I, as Hodge frolicked at the twine, "I knew this cat, Jeoffrey. It was with Kit in the Madhouse, and after. I took them meat, and a blanket. A cat may surely be a servant, more than many men, for he does no wickedness. Are not all the records of man, but narratives of successive villanies, of treasons and usurpations, massacres and wars? Are not all the records of cats and dogs, but narratives of comfort, service and friendship? Yet, there are those that will ever say, 'This is but a cat, or, this but a dog'. Poor Kit very wisely observed this:

> Though these some spirits think but light,
> And deem indifferent things;
> Yet they are serious in the sight
> Of CHRIST, the King of kings...

...an Awful truth upon which many that like not dogs and cats might profitably meditate."

VI

One hater of cats I encountered at the Ivy-Lane Club one night. Boswell was there, and I remember, there were also two gentlemen who practised very uncommon arts. One was Mr. Busby, a proctor of the Commons, who was a most accurate imitator of cats. The other was Mr. Salter of the Charter-House, who could yelp like a hound. They performed extempore a dialogue so ingeniously done it seemed to have meaning, rather than mere mowls and yelps. These are arts that those who ridicule should not so readily despise, since they lighten melancholy and foster friendship. I know not if you drink in inns and coffee-houses, but if you do, then you will know this: there is always one there that will say, "What think you of Aristotle?" - or worse, he will impart, at tedious length, his latest commentary upon the Poetics. Give me rather Busby's mowls and Proctor's yelps.

That night, there was a rake, of noble birth, slender means and effeminate bearing, who versified and called himself a poet. It was known that the rake's wife, a timid creature, had begged if she could but keep a little cat, to gladden her solitary hours with merriment and companionship. Mr. Busby, eager to know if the cat would be procured, pressed him to relate the outcome. "I refused, sir," said the rake in a very languid manner, "for a cat is a useless thing and signifies nothing for a poet." I rebuked him thus: "Depend upon it sir, to a poet nothing can be useless. Whatever is beautiful and whatever is dreadful must be familiar to his imagination; he must be conversant with all that is awfully vast or elegantly little. The plants of the garden, the minerals of the earth, the meteors of the sky and the animals at the hearth, must all concur to store his mind with inexhaustible variety; for every idea is useful for the enforcement or decoration of moral, and indeed religious, truth." This silenced him. And all the others too, till Busby and Salter filled the awful vacuum with mowls and yelps of assent.

Once, this Busby called on Hodge. I was not there, but heard from Mrs. Williams.

"Mr. Busby came," said she.

"What said he?" said I.

"He said 'mow' to Hodge," said she.

"And what said Hodge?" said I.

"Hodge said naught," said she.

"Well then, Madam," said I, "Babies, cats. They do not love our schemes of merriment. Nothing is more hopeless, Mrs. Williams, than a scheme of merriment." [*Settles in armchair.*]

VII

Now Mr. Boswell has an antipathy to cats. He is uneasy when in the room with one, and frequently suffered a good deal from the presence of Hodge, but his kind temperament brought him nobly to disguise this. One day he called at my house while sat here, sporting with Hodge. It was a simple sport, where Hodge fancied me a man-mountain, whereof the summit he would conquer. Each time he gained the upper slopes of my bosom, I whistled in fair imitation of the perilous gusts that blow on lofty peaks - and put him low to try one more ascent [demonstrates, with the doll.] Thus! On observing our enterprise, Boz remarked that Hodge was a fine cat. "Ay sir," said I, "but I have had cats I liked better." That moment, I'd bestowed the traitor's kiss, and fancied Hodge much out of countenance. I swiftly said that Hodge was a fine cat, a very fine cat indeed. I privately consoled myself with another Truth, that it was my habit perpetually to gainsay Mr. Boswell. Should he say "night", let me say "day", though it be the darkest of nights. The knife of wit requires a whetstone, and he was mine.

VIII

When Hodge came to full growth, I daily left open a window, so he might go where he list, an indulgence that I felt was due to him. I fancied that the happy gale of fortune might suddenly waft him into new regions, where unaccustomed lustre might dazzle his eyes, and yet untasted delicacies solicit his appetite. However, he did not roam far and near danger, so I never closed him up, but once, and for this reason. There was a young Gentleman of good family who had tumbled into a despicable state, and was running about town shooting cats. I closed Hodge up, and the same day chanced on Mr. Langton in the Square. I warned him, for he too kept a cat and, I think, a dog.

"Is Hodge secure?" said Langton.

"He is, Sir," said I. "Hodge shan't be shot; no, no: Hodge shall not be shot, for I have closed him up. Look yonder at the window of my house, for there he sits. He perceives us standing here. He cannot comprehend the remedy, so he is sad. But he is safe."

Touching on cruelty to beasts, I met Mr. Hogarth, the painter, at Sam Richardson's one day. He had drawn a most accurate picture, that he shewed me, of wretches in a street. Some boys had hanged two cats by their tails, upon a lamppost that looked like a gibbet. In the street beyond was a high building where a ruffian leered down from an attic. He had tied wings to a cat's back, and tossed him out the window. The cat could be seen in mid-air, a wretched parody of Icarus, and you could but imagine the terrour that attended his descent.

"Saw you this, Sir?" said I.

"It happened in France, Sir," said Hogarth, "where they had a Massacre of Cats."

"Depend on it, Sir," said I, "There are worse horrors yet, awaiting thy ingenious pencil. Among the inferior professors of medical knowledge, is a race of wretches, whose favourite amusement is to nail cats and dogs to tables and open them alive, to examine whether burning irons are felt more acutely by the bone or tendon; and whether the more lasting agonies are produced by poison forced into the mouth, or injected into the veins.

What is alleged in defence of those hateful practices, every one knows; but the truth is, that by knives, fire, and poison, knowledge is not always sought and is very seldom attained. The experiments that have been tried, are tried again; he that burned an animal with irons yesterday, will be willing to amuse himself with burning another tomorrow. He surely buys knowledge dear, who learns it at the expense of his humanity. It is time that universal resentment should arise against these horrid operations, which harden the heart, extinguish those sensations which give man confidence in man, and make the physician more dreadful than the gout or stone."

As to the defenestration of cats, I met at the Mitre Tavern a Mr. Bentham, an ingenious young man who had penned a mockery of the American upstarts and their impudent Declaration of Independence. The talk turned to cats and he told me this. When but a boy he was, though studious at school, ever a prey to the inherent vices of boyhood. Once, he fell to sporting with a cat in his grandmother's room. He had heard the story of cats having nine lives, and being sure of falling on their legs; and thus he threw the cat out of the window on a grass-plot. When it fell, it turned towards him, looked in his face and mewed. "Poor thing!" said he, "thou art reproaching me with my unkindness." He said a servant also chid him for burning earwigs in a candle. An uncle chid him for teasing a dog, named Busy, and fomenting a quarrel between this dog and another. And thus he learned kindness, so when a decayed gentleman came to the house one day, and would shew him the way to imprison flies in a cage of cork and sticks, he liked it not. This Bentham is a man of singular parts. May his genius redound to the betterment of present times, and the adornment of posterity.

And what, I ask you, is to give man confidence in man? The innocence of babes, for sure. One day Mrs. Adams brought her niece, a cheerful little thing not five years old. Hodge proved a willing instrument for this child to practise kindness upon. She stroked his cheeks, and told him she would take him to a palace, like the King's. This palace she described, with a delightful contrariety of images. Without the wall were beating billows, howling storms and dragons. Within were feasts and elegance, beauty and gaiety, song and dance.

There they would live their days, in ease and opulence.

Her aunt then said, "Do not forget the Poor."

"Them too," she brightly said, "them too: they shall live with us."

She then resolved to bring the Poor to Mrs. Adams' house, that very day; all of them, and Hodge.

IX

Hodge, I fear to tell, grew old in time. We must either outlive our friends, you know, or our friends must outlive us. And I see no man that would hesitate about the choice. Any man that has kept a cat or a dog will know this keenly, for these are friends that are the first to pass. Some keep skulls or crosses by them: memento mori. Yet there can be no reminder of mortality so sweet, or so bitter, as the animal we love. As Hodge grew old, he waned by slow degrees. At first his zeal seemed but little diluted, though he gave more time to slumber than to frolick. Later, his teeth were lost to a distemper of his jaw, which caused him pain. At length, his once sprightly limbs propelled him but the shortest distance, though he would sport when able. Finally, he would lie passive in this crib for hours. When he was not overwhelmed by agony, he was lost in dejection.

Every man that has felt pain, knows how few the comforts are that can gladden him to whom health is denied. I fed Hodge valerian to ease his agonies. I bought oysters for his delight, these being soft, and the best meat for his toothless jaws. I went for them myself. I had no wish to humiliate poor Francis by sending him on so shameful an errand, for oysters are cheap and plentiful, and none but the poorest wretches eat them. But were oysters a hundred-fold the price, as they were in Julius Caesar's Rome, I should have found gold to procure them for poor Hodge, as he loved them.

One morning I walked to Porridge-island, a mean street by St Martin-in-the-Fields, where there are cook-shops and carts for the poor. A small mob clustered round the oyster carts, and I was forced to wait while they dispersed. The day was gloomy. It began to rain. I thought of a darker morning, some three-score years ago, when I was a small boy, and refused to go with my father to Uttoxeter Market, where he sold books from a mean stall. Pride was the source of this refusal, and the remembrance of it was ever painful. Not long ago I desired to atone for this fault, and went to Uttoxeter. An old man now, I stood for a considerable time, bareheaded, in the rain, on the spot where my father's stall used to stand. In contrition I stood, and I hoped the penance was expiatory, but felt it not. Now, at the oyster cart in Porridge-island, I felt myself absolved, and this was no mere fancy. What we seek is very seldom found where it is sought. Our brightest blaze of gladness is commonly kindled by unexpected sparks. So it was that oyster day, in the cold rain of London.

There was frolic in Hodge when I returned. Presently, the sun shone, and so I carried him into the Square. He tried his ball of twine a while, then sate upon my knees. I rubbed on Hodge's cheeks, which made him smile and rumble. Boswell came, we found some merriment. A rainbow came, and the bright bells of St Brides pealed at six, and when they did, Hodge fell asleep, and never woke again. I took him back and laid him here.

X

Francis, unbidden, made a box for him, and lined it with some stuff of my old brown coat, that Hodge had always lain on. I put him in. I said a prayer. I wept.

Of course, Mrs. Knowles and Mrs. Adams loved poor Hodge. They came to the house next morning to dispense comfort and take refreshment. Hodge lay in his casket on this table, while I stood despondently upon the hearth, rolling about as I sometimes do, with no doubt a serious, solemn, and somewhat gloomy air. Mrs. Knowles said what an affecting funeral this was, to remember a poor cat that was one of God's creatures.

"Every funeral, madam," I said, reposing my hand on my friend's casket, "be it a cat's or a king's, may justly be considered as a summons to prepare for that state we must sometime enter; and the summons is more loud and piercing, as the evening of which it warns us is at less distance. To neglect at any time preparation for death, is to sleep on our post at a siege, but to omit it in old age, is to sleep at an attack."

This did not silence her. This day, Mrs.

Knowles seemed driven by the persuasion of divine light.

"Nay," she said, "thou should'st not have such a horrour for what is the gate of Life. Does not St. Paul say, 'I have fought the good fight of faith, I have finished my course; henceforth is laid up for me a crown of life'?"

"Ay, Madam," I said, "but St. Paul was a man inspired, a man who had been converted by supernatural interposition."

Mrs. Adams then reproached me. "You seem, Sir, to forget the merits of our Redeemer."

"Madam," said I, "I do not forget the merits of my Redeemer; but my Redeemer has said that he will set some on his right hand, and some on his left."

I assumed a look of stern agitation, no hard task, but said, more softly, "I'll have no more on it, no more on it." For they were kind ladies. Very kind ladies indeed.

Later that day, we interred dear Hodge in the shade of Mr. Thrale's old apple tree, near the Mansion House. The sunlight dappled the orchard, and a solitary bird sat tuning upon a branch. I reflected, not for the last time, how the shepherd in

Virgil grew at last acquainted with love, and found him a native of the rocks. But at length such gloom was dispelled, by the bells of St. Brides, joyfully calling.

EPILOGUE

Thank you for your company, dear friends. I have lately seemed to myself broken off from mankind; a kind of solitary wanderer in the wild of life, without any direction, or fixed point of view: a gloomy gazer on a world to which I have little relation. And now you have supplied that want of closer union, by friendship. Let us think of one another this night, and consider our sufferings as notices, mercifully given us to prepare ourselves for another state. Let us be thankful for one another, and for our cats and dogs, and families and friends. The world passes away, and we are passing with it; but there is, doubtless, another world, which will endure for ever. [*Music opens, the Ballad again, quiet at first but steadily swelling* .] Be it another life, or be it an eternal extinction of all our troubles, let us be of good cheer, and fit ourselves for whatever may be to come. Come, Francis! [*Bangs fist decisively on*

the table.] Let us go forth and breakfast in splen-
dour! [*Music swells, slow blackout as Johnson exits.*]

CURTAIN

APPENDIX I

An Elegy on The Death of Dr Johnson's Favourite Cat

by Percival Stockdale

Percival Stockdale (1736–1811) was an English poet, writer and reformer. After a spell in the army, serving with the Royal Welch Fusiliers, he took holy orders in 1759. Had he lived to see it, Johnson might well have been impressed by Stockdale's spirited reaction to the Haitian Revolution of 1792. This "insurrection of the negroes", to use Johnson's phrase, was the largest uprising of slaves since the rebellion of Spartacus against the Roman Republic. Stockdale, along with fellow abolitionist William Roscoe, defended the atrocities that the Haitian rebels inflicted on their French oppressors. Sadly, as poet and critic, Stockdale never gained the respect he felt he deserved. His *Memoirs*, seldom read today, form for the most part a depressing litany of self-pity, jealousy and delusion. Notable works remain, however, some of which deserve to be revisited. A good example is *A Remonstrance against Inhumanity to Animals, and particularly against the Savage Practice of Bull-Baiting* (Alnwick, 1802), a significant work written at a time when coherent thinking on animal rights was very much in its infancy. Stockdale's relationship with Johnson blew hot and cold, especially since the fateful moment when Johnson was chosen to write *Lives of the Poets*, a commission Stockdale had confidently expected for himself. Nonetheless, he managed to remain on congenial terms with Hodge, if not always with Johnson, as witnessed by this charming poem.

Let not the honest muse disdain
For Hodge to wake the plaintive strain.
Shall poets prostitute their lays
In offering venal Statesmen praise;
By them shall flowers Parnassian bloom
Around the tyrant's gaudy tomb;

And shall not Hodge's memory claim
Of innocence the candid fame;
Shall not his worth a poem fill,
Who never thought, nor uttered ill;
Who by his manner when caressed
Warmly his gratitude expressed;
And never failed his thanks to purr
Whene'er he stroaked his sable furr?
The general conduct if we trace
Of our articulating race,
Hodge's, example we shall find
A keen reproof of human kind.
He lived in town, yet ne'er got drunk,
Nor spent one farthing on a punk;
He never filched a single groat,
Nor bilked a taylor of a coat;
His garb when first he drew his breath
His dress through life, his shroud in death.
Of human speech to have the power,
To move on two legs, not on four;
To view with unobstructed eye
The verdant field, the azure sky
Favoured by luxury to wear
The velvet gown, the golden glare -
If honour from these gifts we claim,

Chartres had too severe a fame.
But wouldst though, son of Adam, learn
Praise from thy noblest powers to earn;
Dost thou, with generous pride aspire
Thy nature's glory to acquire?
Then in thy life exert the man,
With moral deed adorn the span;
Let virtue in they bosom lodge;
Or wish thou hadst been born a Hodge.

APPENDIX II

Dr Johnson and Hodge His Cat

by Susan Coolidge (Sarah Chauncey Woolsey)

Sarah Chauncey Woolsey (1835–1905) was an American children's author who wrote under the pen name Susan Coolidge. She is best known for her children's novels *What Katy Did*, *What Katy Did at School*, and *What Katy Did Next*. The central character, Katy, is based on Woolsey herself and the other children on her siblings. In all she wrote some forty books, most of them directed at young female readers. *Just Sixteen*, *Not Quite Eighteen*, and *An Old Convent School in Paris* are indicative examples of the output. There are agreeable and unexpected surprises, such as *A Short History of the City of Philadelphia from its foundation to the present time* (1887) and 'A group of New England dishes furnished by Susan Coolidge', included in Mary Ronald's *Century Cook Book* (1897). Woolsey also wrote many children's stories and poems for publication in the magazines of the day. A good example is 'How Bunny Brought Good Luck', a gripping tale of how the loss of a toy rabbit leads to the discovery of a valuable silver mine. Dr. Johnson and Hodge His Cat, probably the finest Horatian ode ever to emerge from Newport, Rhode Island, first appeared in the *United Presbyterian Youth Evangelist Paper* (No. 28, July 12, 1903).

Burly and big, his books among,
Good Samuel Johnson sat,
With frowning brows and wig askew,
His snuff-strewn waistcoat far from new;
So stern and menacing his air,
That neither Black Sam,
nor the maid
To knock or interrupt him dare;
Yet close beside him, unafraid,
Sat Hodge, the cat.

"This participle," the Doctor wrote,
"The modern scholar cavils at,
But," - even as he penned the word,
A soft, protesting note was heard;
The Doctor fumbled with his pen,
The dawning thought took wings and flew,
The sound repeated, come again,
It was a faint, reminding "Mew!"
From Hodge, the cat...

The Dictionary was laid down,
The Doctor tied his vast cravat,
And down the buzzing street he strode,
Taking an often-trodden road,
And halted at a well-known stall:
"Fishmonger," spoke the Doctor gruff,
"Give me six oysters, that is all;
Hodge knows when he has had enough,
Hodge is my cat."

Then home; puss dined and while in sleep
he chased a visionary rat,
His master sat him down again,
Rewrote his page, renibbed his pen;

Each "i" was dotted, each "t" was crossed,
He labored on for all to read,
Nor deemed that time was waste or lost
Spent in supplying the small need
Of Hodge, the cat.

The dear old Doctor! Fierce of mien,
Untidy, arbitrary, fat,
What gentle thought his name enfold!
So generous of his scanty gold.
So quick to love, so hot to scorn,
Kind to all sufferers under heaven,
A tend'rer despot ne'er was born;
His big heart held a corner, even
For Hodge, the cat.

APPENDIX III

From 'The Cat by the Fire'

by Leigh Hunt

James Henry Leigh Hunt (1784 – 28), known as Leigh Hunt, was an English critic, essayist and poet. He is remembered for his impressively wide circle of acquaintance in the literary world and for having played an important part in establishing the reputations of Keats, Shelley, Byron, Browning and Tennyson. After a short career as a clerk in the War Office, in 1808 he was appointed editor of *The Examiner*, a radical magazine founded by his brother John. Another brother, Robert, also contributed to the magazine, which quickly became known for its anti-establishment views and coruscating editorial. Two notable figures were among the many attacked in its pages. One was William Blake, whom Leigh Hunt dismissed as a "quack" and whose work Robert

Hunt described as "the ebullitions of a distempered brain". Blake mounted a robust counterattack, describing the Hunt brothers and their team as a "nest of villains". Another target was the Prince Regent himself, whom Hunt described as "a corpulent man of fifty", "a violator of his word", without "a single claim on the gratitude of his people or the respect of posterity". This proved too much for the British Government, who prosecuted the Hunts for seditious libel in 1813. They were sent to prison, in Leigh's case for two years. However, his time in Surrey County Gaol turned out to be very agreeable. He decorated his cell with pretty wallpaper and the genial governor allowed him various luxuries, including a garden, a piano, a bust of Homer and a servant. More important, he continued to write articles for *The Examiner* during his sentence and inevitably became widely admired as a martyr in the cause of liberty and freedom of speech. This excerpt from 'The Cat by the fire' is a good example of his easy and somewhat whimsical prose style.

And this reminds us of an exquisite anecdote of dear, dogmatic, diseased, thoughtful, surly, charitable Johnson, who would go out of doors himself, and buy oysters for his cat, because his black servant was too proud to do it! But Johnson's true practical delicacy in the matter is beautiful. Be assured that he thought nothing of "condescension" in it, or of being eccentric. He was singular in some things, because he could not help it. But he hated eccentricity. No: in his best moments he felt himself simply to be a man, and a good man too, though a frail—one that in virtue as well as humility, and in a knowledge of his ignorance as well as his wisdom, was desirous of being a Christian philosopher; and accordingly he went out, and bought food for his hungry cat, because his poor negro was too proud to do it, and there was nobody else in the way whom he had a right to ask. What must anybody that saw him have thought, as he turned up Bolt Court! But doubtless he went as secretly as possible—that is to say, if he considered the thing at all. His friend Garrick could not have done as much! He was too grand, and on the great "stage" of life. Goldsmith could; but he would hardly have thought of it. Beauclerc might; but he would have thought it necessary to excuse it with a jest or a wager, or some such thing. Sir Joshua Reynolds, with his fashionable, fine-lady-painting hand, would certainly have shrunk from it. Burke would have reasoned himself into its propriety, but he would have reasoned himself out again. Gibbon! Imagine its being put into the head of Gibbon! He and his bag-wig would have started with all the horror of a gentleman-usher; and he would have rung the bell for the cook's-deputy's-under-assistant-errand-boy.

APPENDIX IV

Jeoffry (from *Jubilate Agno*)

by Christopher Smart

Christopher Smart (1722–1771) was an English poet. He is remembered chiefly for his religious works, although he had other interests including botany, natural sciences and taxonomy, all of which are evident in the themes and structure of his poetry. Jeoffry plays a cameo role a much larger poem, *Jubilate Agno*, which Smart wrote when he was confined in St Luke's Hospital for Lunatics at the instigation of his father-in-law and publisher, John Newbery. Newbery's motives remain debatable. It is certainly true that he found Smart's increasingly erratic behaviour extremely irritating, not to mention his rather bewildering dual personality. On the one hand Smart was an accomplished classical scholar, and a devout Christian, whose religious poetry was bright with reverence and celebration. On the other he was a serial debtor with a history of recklessness dating back to his undergraduate days at Oxford. Furthermore, in addition to his failure to provide a secure income for his wife and family, he had also taken to preaching inflammatory sermons in public. Whatever the reasons for it, his confinement in St Luke's was redeemed by the creation of two important works, *A Song of David* and *Jubilate Agno*. The central idea of *Jubilate Agno* is perhaps that all Creation, including Jeoffry, is engaged in a perpetual act of worship that it is the poet's task to celebrate and articulate. The poem runs to 1200 lines, but it is the 854 words devoted to Jeoffry that have kept Smart's memory alive for the general reader. The passage is a miniature masterpiece, a bright point in an otherwise troubled and unhappy life.

For I will consider my Cat Jeoffry.

For he is the servant of the Living God duly and daily serving him.

For at the first glance of the glory of God in the East he worships in his way.

For this is done by wreathing his body seven times round with elegant quickness.

For then he leaps up to catch the musk, which is the blessing of God upon his prayer.

For he rolls upon prank to work it in.

For having done duty and received blessing he begins to consider himself.

For this he performs in ten degrees.

For first he looks upon his forepaws to see if they are clean.

For secondly he kicks up behind to clear away there.

For thirdly he works it upon stretch with the forepaws extended.

For fourthly he sharpens his paws by wood.

For fifthly he washes himself.

For sixthly he rolls upon wash.

For seventhly he fleas himself, that he may not be interrupted upon the beat.

For eighthly he rubs himself against a post.

For ninthly he looks up for his instructions.

For tenthly he goes in quest of food.

For having consider'd God and himself he will consider his neighbour.

For if he meets another cat he will kiss her in kindness.

For when he takes his prey he plays with it to give it a chance.

For one mouse in seven escapes by his dallying.

For when his day's work is done his business more properly begins.

For he keeps the Lord's watch in the night against the adversary.

For he counteracts the powers of darkness by his electrical skin and glaring eyes.

For he counteracts the Devil, who is death, by brisking about the life.

For in his morning orisons he loves the sun and the sun loves him.

For he is of the tribe of Tiger.

For the Cherub Cat is a term of the Angel Tiger.

For he has the subtlety and hissing of a serpent, which in goodness he suppresses.

For he will not do destruction, if he is well-fed, neither will he spit without provocation.

For he purrs in thankfulness, when God tells him he's a good Cat.

For he is an instrument for the children to learn benevolence upon.

For every house is incomplete without him and a blessing is lacking in the spirit.

For the Lord commanded Moses concerning the cats at the departure of the Children of Israel from Egypt.

For every family had one cat at least in the bag.

For the English Cats are the best in Europe.

For he is the cleanest in the use of his forepaws of any quadruped.

For the dexterity of his defence is an instance of the love of God to him exceedingly.

For he is the quickest to his mark of any creature.

For he is tenacious of his point.

For he is a mixture of gravity and waggery.

For he knows that God is his Saviour.

For there is nothing sweeter than his peace when at rest.

For there is nothing brisker than his life when in motion.

For he is of the Lord's poor and so indeed is he called by benevolence perpetually—Poor Jeoffry! poor Jeoffry! the rat has bit thy throat.

For I bless the name of the Lord Jesus that Jeoffry is better.

For the divine spirit comes about his body to sustain it in complete cat.

For his tongue is exceeding pure so that it has in purity what it wants in music.

For he is docile and can learn certain things.

For he can set up with gravity which is patience upon approbation.

For he can fetch and carry, which is patience in employment.

For he can jump over a stick which is patience upon proof positive.

For he can spraggle upon waggle at the word of command.

For he can jump from an eminence into his master's bosom.

For he can catch the cork and toss it again.

For he is hated by the hypocrite and miser.
For the former is afraid of detection.

For the latter refuses the charge.

For he camels his back to bear the first notion of business.

For he is good to think on, if a man would express himself neatly.

For he made a great figure in Egypt for his signal services.

For he killed the Ichneumon-rat very pernicious by land.

For his ears are so acute that they sting again.

For from this proceeds the passing quickness of his attention.

For by stroking of him I have found out electricity.

For I perceived God's light about him both wax and fire.

For the Electrical fire is the spiritual substance, which God sends from heaven to sustain the bodies both of man and beast.

For God has blessed him in the variety of his movements.

For, tho he cannot fly, he is an excellent clamberer.

For his motions upon the face of the earth are more than any other quadruped.

For he can tread to all the measures upon the music.

For he can swim for life.

For he can creep.

APPENDIX V

Jeremy Bentham

Jeremy Bentham (1748–1832) was an English philosopher, jurist and social reformer. He was the founding father of modern utilitarianism, a doctrine built on his axiom that "it is the greatest happiness of the greatest number that is the measure of right and wrong". Bentham is also widely remembered for his lifelong commitment to prison reform and for his views on animal rights. As regards animals, Bentham strongly opposed the prevailing view, advanced by Descartes and others, that animals were mere automata, complex but soulless machines, incapable of thought or feeling, disqualified from protection within the moral and ethical framework that shelters man. Bentham disagreed: "...the question is not, Can they reason? nor, Can they talk? but, Can they suffer?

Why should the law refuse its protection to any sensitive being? The time will come when humanity will extend its mantle over everything which breathes." The following excerpts are taken from Bentham's recollections of his early childhood. It seems clear from Bentham's tone that these episodes, all of them involving animals, were profoundly formative.

The Earwigs: "We had a servant, whose name was Martha: a woman of kindness and gentleness; and the kindness of her temper ameliorated mine. One day, while I was a little boy, I went into the kitchen. Some earwigs were running about. I laid hold of them, and put them into the candle. Martha gave me a sharp rebuke, and asked me, how I should like to be so used myself? The rebuke was not thrown away."

The Cat: "From my youth I was fond of cats—as I still am. I was once playing with one in my grandmother's room. I had heard the story of cats having nine lives, and being sure of falling on their legs; and I threw the cat out of the window on the grass-plot. When it fell, it turned towards me, looked in my face and mewed. 'Poor thing!' I said, 'thou art reproaching me with my unkindness.' I have a distinct recollection of all these things."

The Dog: "My uncle's house, in Hampshire, was the scene of a very useful lesson. A personage, of no small importance in the family, was a dog named Busy. He was a model of the conjunction of fidelity and surliness. A very slight cause sufficed to elicit from him a loud and long-continued growl. No beggar durst approach the house. I myself stood in no inconsiderable awe of him. One day I thought to find amusement in fomenting a quarrel between him and another dog. While I was thus employed up came my uncle, and reprimanded me for my cruelty. I felt it bitterly; for it was the only token of displeasure I ever experienced from him, from the day of my earliest recollection to the day of his death, which took place in 1784. He was one of the gentlest of all human beings, though a lawyer by profession."

The Flies: "A neighbouring decayed gentleman, of the name of Vernon, came to pay a morning visit to my grandmother. By way of recommending himself to my favour, he brought with him, in his pocket, a toy of his own manufacture. It was a cage for the reception of flies, formed by two horizontal slices of cork connected together by uprights composed of pins. All but one were fixed—that one was moveable—and the amusement consisted in catching the miserable animals and cramming them into the cage, till it would hold no more. Sometimes they got in with all their limbs; sometimes with one or all, or any number between one and all, torn off. When I had amused myself with the instrument for some minutes, a train of reflection came across me; the result was an abhorrence of the invention, coupled with a feeling not far short of abhorrence for the inventor and donor."

POUSSIN PUBLICATIONS

Paris

MMXX

Ingram Content Group UK Ltd.
Milton Keynes UK
UKHW040734240423
420680UK00001B/214